# The Ultimate Kids
# Joke Book

# The Ultimate Kids Joke Book

The Laugh-Out-Loud Gift for Kids with Jokes,
Knock Knock Jokes for Kids,
and More!

An imprint of Penguin Random House LLC
1745 Broadway
New York, New York 10014
penguinrandomhouse.com

This volume first published 2018
First published by Joke Books for Kids, an imprint of
Penguin Random House LLC, 2018
Copyright © 2018 by Penguin Random House

Jokes used with permission from funkidsjokes.com

ISBN: 9781984877154

Printed in the United States of America
1 3 5 7 9 10 8 6 4 2

Book Design By: North Market Street Graphics
Cover Design By: Meredith Snyder
Cover/Interior Art by: doshi_do/Shutterstock

# Contents

# 1

# Knock Knock!

Knock, knock.
Who's there?
Algy.
Algy who?
Algy-bra.

Knock, knock.
Who's there?
Bass.
Bass who?
Bass-ball is my favorite sport.

Knock, knock.
Who's there?
Buckle.
Buckle who?
Buckle get you an ice cream cone.

Knock, knock.
Who's there?
Felix.
Felix who?
Felix my ice cream, I'm telling.

Knock, knock.
Who's there?
Ferret.
Ferret who?
Ferret the ferr-grounds every summer.

Knock, knock.
Who's there?
Flicker.
Flicker who?
Flicker ice cream she'll get mad.

Knock, knock.

Who's there?

Francoise.

Francoise who?

Francoise where I went on vacation.


Knock, knock.

Who's there?

Hank.

Hank who?

Hankerin' for some ice cream.


Knock, knock.

Who's there?

Henrietta.

Henrietta who?

Henrietta too much ice cream and threw up.


Knock, knock.

Who's there?

Ice cream.

Ice cream who?

Ice cream at scary movies.

Knock, knock.

Who's there?

Ice cream.

Ice cream who?

Ice cream if you don't let me in.

Knock, knock.

Who's there?

Ice cream.

Ice cream who?

Ice cream soda whole class can hear me.

Knock, knock.

Who's there?

Banana.

Banana who?

Knock, knock.

Who's there?

Banana.

Banana who?

Knock, knock.

Who's there?

Orange.

Orange who?

Orange you glad I didn't say banana again?

Knock, knock.
Who's there?
Soccer.
Soccer who?
Socc-ser in the drawer.

Knock, knock.
Who's there?
Tennis.
Tennis who?
Tennis my favorite number!

Knock, knock.
Who's there?
Worm.
Worm who?
Worm in here, isn't it?

Knock, knock.
Who's there?
Bach.
Bach who?
Bach, bach, bach—I'm a chicken.

Knock, knock.
Who's there?
Uriah.
Uriah who?
Keep Uriah on the ball.

Knock, knock.
Who's there?
Fonda.
Fonda who?
Fonda you!

Knock, knock.
Who's there?
Frank.
Frank who?
Frank you for being my friend.

Knock, knock.
Who's there?
Gracie.
Gracie who?
Gracie about you.

Knock, knock.
Who's there?
Heart.
Heart who?
Heart knocks life.

Knock, knock.
Who's there?
Holmes.
Holmes who?
Holmes is where the heart is.

Knock, knock.
Who's there?
Iguana.
Iguana who?
Iguana hold your hand.

Knock, knock.
Who's there?
Iris.
Iris who?
Iris you were here.

Knock, knock.
Who's there?
Pooch.
Pooch who?
Pooch your arms around me.

Knock, knock.
Who's there?
Beru.
Beru who?
Don't cry . . .

Knock, knock.
Who's there?
Hip.
Hip who?
It's not hipwho, it's hippo!

Knock, knock.
Who's There?
You Know.
You Know Who?
That's right, I do!

Knock, knock.
Who's there?
Hoo.
Hoo who?
Hoo Hoo Hoo Hoo!

Knock, knock.
Who's there?
Owl.
Owl who?
Owl at the moon.

Knock, knock.
Who's there?
Tut.
Tut who?
Tut, tut it looks like rain.

Knock, knock.
Who's there?
Leia.
Leia who?
Leia cookie on my plate.

# 2

# Amazing Animal Jokes

Father: Why are you crying?

Son: Because I wanted to get a dinosaur for my baby sister.

Father: That's no reason to cry . . .

Son: Yes it is—nobody would trade me for her!

Knock, knock.

Who's there?

Candy.

Candy who?

Candy cow jump over the moon?

Q: Did you hear about the snobby cow?
A: She thought she was a cutlet above the rest.

Q: How did the cow get to Mars?
A: It flew through udder space.

Q: How do baby chickens dance?
A: Chick-to-chick.

Q: How do chickens bake cakes?
A: From scratch.

Q: How do chickens send letters?
A: In hen-velopes.

Q: How do dogs stop a dvd?
A: They press the paws button.

Q: How do you get a cow to keep quiet?
A: Press the moooote button.

Q: How do you know it's cold outside?
A: When you milk a brown cow and you get chocolate ice cream.

Q: How do you know when a chicken has been arrested?
A: It's wearing hencuffs.

Q: How long do chickens work?
A: Around the cluck.

Q: If fruit comes from a fruit tree, where would a chicken come from?

A: A poul-tree.

Q: Since chickens rise when the rooster crows, when do ducks wake up?

A: At the quack of dawn.

Q: What did the dog say to the hippopotamus?

A: Woof.

Q: What did the mommy cow say to the baby cow?

A: It's pasture bedtime!

Q: What direction do chickens swim?

A: Cluck-wise.

Q: What do chicken comedians tell?

A: Funny yolks.

Q: What do chickens grow on?

A: Eggplants.

Q: What do chickens say when you try to charge them?

A: Put it on my bill.

Q: What do chickens serve at birthday parties?

A: Coop cakes.

Q: What do marathon running chickens need most?

A: Hendurance.

Q: What do you call a bird that's scared of flying?
A: A chicken.

Q: What do you call a chicken that tells jokes?
A: A comedi-hen.

Q: What do you call a chicken with a piece of lettuce in it's eye?
A: Chicken Caeser Salad.

Q: What do you call a cow who trips in a corn field?
A: Corned beef.

Q: What do you call a crazy chicken?
A: A cuckoo cluck.

Q: What do you call a group of chickens clucking a song together?
A: A Hensemble.

Q: What do you call a haunting chicken?
A: A poultry-geist.

Q: What do you call an explosive egg?
A: A bombshell.

Q: What do you call cattle that tell jokes?
A: Laughing stock.

Q: What do you call it when it rains chickens and ducks?
A: Fowl weather.

Q: What do you call it when you cross a dinosaur with a pig?

A: Jurassic pork!

Q: What do you call someone who steals chicken at sea?

A: A chicken pot pirate.

Q: What do you get from an Eskimo cow?

A: Ice cream.

Q: What do you get if you cross a farm animal with a map maker?

A: A cow-tographer.

Q: What do you get when you cross a chicken with a cow?

A: Roost beef.

Q: What do you get when you cross a cow and a duck?

A: Milk and quackers!

Q: What do you get when you mix a transformer with a cow?

A: Optimus prime rib.

Q: What does a chicken wipe it's beak with?

A: A henkerchief.

Q: What does a mixed-up hen lay?

A: Scrambled eggs.

Q: What happened to the chicken who found a four-leaf clover?

A: He had good cluck forever.

Q: What time do chickens go to lunch?

A: About twelve o'cluck.

Q: When is chicken soup not good for your health?

A: When you're the chicken.

Q: Where do tough chickens come from?

A: Hard-boiled eggs.

Q: Which chicken is most ruthless?

A: Attila the Hen.

Q: Which dance will a chicken never do?

A: The foxtrot.

Q: Which day of the week do chickens hate most?

A: Fry-day.

Q: Which holy man do chickens dread most?

A: Friars.

Q: Which is the biggest cow in the world that doesn't give milk?

A: Moscow.

Q: Why are chickens such bad umpires?

A: They always call fowl balls.

Q: Why could the chicken only lay eggs during the winter?

A: She was no spring chicken.

Q: Why did half the chicken cross the road?
A: To get to its other side.

Q: Why did the cactus cross the road?
A: It was stuck to the chicken.

Q: Why did the chicken cross the playground?
A: To get to the other slide.

Q: Why did the chicken cross the road twice?
A: He was a double-crosser.

Q: Why did the chicken cross the road?
A: Just Beakause.

Q: Why did the chicken get ejected from the baseball game?

A: For persistent fowl play.

Q: Why did the chicken go to the seance?

A: To get to the other side.

Q: Why did the chicken join a band?

A: Because it already had the drumsticks.

Q: Why did the Roman hen cross the road?

A: She was worried someone would Caesar.

Q: Why did the rooster run away?

A: He was chicken.

Q: Why did the rubber chicken cross the road?
A: To stretch it's legs.

Q: Why didn't the chicken skeleton cross the road?
A: He didn't have enough guts.

Q: Why do chicken families visit parks?
A: To go on peck-nics.

Q: Why do roosters watch TV?
A: For hentertainment.

Q: Why does a chicken coop have two doors?
A: Four doors would make it a chicken sedan.

Q: Why don't cows remember things you tell them?
A: Because everything goes in one ear and out the udder.

Q: How do a cows add?
A: With cow-culators.

Q: How do cows reach sums?
A: By adding one number to an udder one.

Q: How does a chicken tell time?
A: They look at the cluck.

Q: What do you get when you cross a chicken and a centipede?
A: Drumsticks for everyone!

Q: Why did the judge cross the road?
A: Because the chicken was out of order.

Q: Why did the toad hop across the road?
A: He was following the chicken.

Woman: "Why does your daughter say 'cluck, cluck, cluck'?"
Father: "Because she thinks she's a chicken."
Woman: "Why don't you tell her that she's not a chicken?"
Father: "Because we need the eggs."

# 3

# Around the World

Q: Which U.S. state is the smartest?

A: Alabama—it has four A's and one B.

Q: What is the capital of Alaska?

A: Don't Juneau this one?

Q: What is in the center of America?
A: The letter R.

Q: What do penguins wear on their heads?
A: Ice caps.

Q: Who was the penguin's favorite aunt?
A: Aunt Arctica.

Q: Where do sheep go on holiday cruises?
A: To the baaaa-hamas.

Q: What soccer team do sheep's like most?
A: FC Baaaaaaa-rcelona!

Q: When does a British tennis match end?
A: When it's Wimble-DONE.

Q: What sort of pudding roams wild in Canada?
A: Mousse (moose).

Q: What did Delaware?
A: Her New Jersey.

Q: What is the biggest mark in the world?
A: Denmark.

Q: What do you call someone from Detroit who talks too much?
A: A Motor-City mouth.

Q: In what way does a moon rock taste different than an Earth rock?

A: It's a little meteor.

Q: What type of rocks do young geologists play with?

A: Marbles.

Q: What is the most romantic city in England?

A: Loverpool.

Q: Which rope is the biggest in the world?

A: Europe.

Q: If dolphins lived on land, which country would they live in?

A: Finland.

Q: Why does it take so long to get into Florida?
A: Because there are so many keys to go through.

Q: Where do pianists go for a vacation?
A: The Florida Keys.

Q: What did the French skeleton slider call his friend?
A: Bone ami.

Q: What do French skeleton teams say to each other before they start eating?
A: Bone appetite.

Q: What patriotic day do French sheep celebrate?
A: Baaaaa-stile Day.

Q: Where do ants go for a vacation?
A: Frants.

Q: Who is the most famous French ant?
A: Napoleant.

Q: What is the most popular dessert for teachers in Georgia?
A: Peach pi.

Q: Why don't you see penguins in Great Britain?
A: Because they're afraid of Wales.

Q: Why was the ninja kicked out of Hollywood?
A: For throwing stars!

Q: How do they describe the Iowa State fair?
A: It's like a corn-ival.

Q: What do you call an Irish spider?
A: Paddy long legs.

Q: What is the most polite building in the world?
A: The leaning tower of Please-a.

Q: What U.S. state has the most math teachers?
A: Mathachussets.

Q: What do they call the city without any small apples?
A: Mini-apple-less.

Q: What do you call a teapot of boiling water on top of Mount Everest?

A: A high-pot-in-use.

Q: What U.S. state is best at producing cheese?

A: Swiss-consin!

Q: What is the capital of Washington?

A: W.

Q: Which state does the most laundry?

A: WASHington.

Q: What is the happiest state in the United States?

A: Merry-land.

Q: Which city has a lot of sand?
A: Sand Francisco.

Q: Where do pencils come from?
A: Pennsylvania.

Q: What's in the middle of Paris?
A: The letter R.

Q: Which tower couldn't fit any more people inside?
A: The I Full Tower.

Q: What has 5 eyes and is lying on the water?
A: The Mississippi River.

Q: What has four eyes but still can't see?
A: Mississippi.

Q: Who was Mississippi married too?
A: Mister Sippi.

Q: Did you hear about Italy?
A: It got Hungary, ate Turkey, slipped on Greece, went shopping in Iceland and then got eaten by Wales.

Q: Which transformer lives in Maine?
A: OptiMoose Prime.

Q: Which U.S. state do lions like the most?
A: Maine.

Q: What's snack is the most popular among teachers in Maine?
A: Whoopie Pi.

Q: How do Mexican sheep say Merry Christmas?
A: Fleece Navidad.

Q: What Jersey rock band do skeleton riders like most?
A: Bone Jovi.

Q: Where do a football players go when they need a new uniform?
A: New Jersey.

Q: Which hockey team do demons root for?
A: The New Jersey Devils.

Q: Why are New Jersey Devils hockey players so fit?

A: It's from all the exorcising.

Q: Where do New Yorkers buy gifts?

A: Yankee Candle.

Q: What is Frankenstein's favorite baseball team?

A: The Frankees.

Q: What do you call fifty penguins at the North Pole?

A: Really lost, because penguins live in the Southern Hemisphere.

Q: What kind of hippos live at the North Pole?

A: Really cold ones.

Q: What's big, furry, white and always points North?

A: A Polar Bearing.

Q: Where is it always 90 degrees, but never hot?

A: The North and South Poles.

# 4

# Arrr You Ready to Giggle

Q: How did the pirate become a lawyer?

A: He passed the barrrrrrr exam.

Q: How did the pirate stop computer hackers?

A: He installed a patch.

Q: How do pirates make money?
A: By hook or by crook.

Q: How do pirates measure the distance they swim?
A: In YARRRRRds.

Q: How do you save a drowning pirate?
A: With C-P-ARRRRRRRRR.

Q: How does a pirate get down from the mast?
A: He can't—you get down from a goose.

Q: How much did the pirate's peg leg and hook cost?
A: An arm and a leg.

Q: How much do pirates charge to pierce someone's ears?
A: A buck an ear.

Q: How much does a pirate pay for corn?
A: A buccaneer.

Q: How much does a pirate's treasure cost?
A: An arm and a leg.

Q: What are a pirate's favorite letters of the alphabet?
A: Arrrrrr and Sea (R and C)

Q: What are pirate children afraid of?
A: The darrrrrrrrrk.

Q: What are the only notes a pirate can sing?
A: High C's.

Q: What did the fruit pirate wear over his eye?
A: A strawberry patch.

Q: What did the pirate do the day before Halloween?
A: Mow his front yarrrrrd.

Q: What did the pirate ninja say to the buccaneer?
A: Ninjarrrrrrrrrgh.

Q: What did the pirate say during a Halloween snow storm?
A: Shiver me timbers.

Q: What did the pirate say during the winter storm?
A: Thar she snows!

Q: What did the pirate's parrot say when it fell in love with a duck?
A: Polly wants a quacker.

Q: What do pirates put on their toast?
A: Jelly Roger.

Q: What do pirates do for fun?
A: Have parrrrrrrrrties.

Q: What do pirates do on Black Friday?
A: Shop the sails.

Q: What do pirates eat on cold winter nights?

A: Hearrrrrrrrrrty stews.

Q: What do pirates order at Italian restaurants?

A: Chicken Parrrrrmesan with spaghetti.

Q: What do pirates think happens at the end of time?

A: Arrrrmageddon.

Q: What do you call a pirate with three eyes?

A: A piiirate.

Q: What do you call a pirate's hair style?

A: A crew cut.

Q: What do you get when you cross a parrot with a shark?
A: An animal that can talk your head off.

Q: What does a gourmet pirate add to the plate to make it look nice?
A: A Garrrrrrr-nish.

Q: What exercise do pirates use to tighten their abs?
A: Planks.

Q: What is a pirates favorite color?
A: Gold!

Q: What job did the pirate have after he quit?
A: He became an arrrrrrchitect.

Q: What kind of socks do pirates wear?

A: Arrrrgghyle socks.

Q: What restaurant do pirates like to eat at the most?

A: The Harrrrrrd Rock Cafe.

Q: What shivers at the bottom of the ocean?

A: A nervous wreck.

Q: What style of food do pirates like the most?

A: Barrrrrrrr-B-Que.

Q: What's the worst thing about cleaning a pirate ship?

A: The barrrrrrnacles.

Q: What type of apple do pirates always look for?
A: Jonagold.

Q: What was the name of Blackbeard's wife?
A: Peg.

Q: What was the name of the pirate's spotted dog?
A: Patches.

Q: What was the pirate captain's favorite restaurant?
A: Jolly Roger.

Q: What was the pirate's favorite food?
A: Arrrrrtichokes.

Q: What was the pirate's favorite Halloween noise maker?

A: Parrrrrrty poppers.

Q: What was the pirate's favorite school subject?

A: Arrrrrrrrrrrrrrrrrrrt.

Q: What was the pirate's favorite U.S. state?

A: Arrrrkansas.

Q: Where do pirates buy pencils and sketch pads?

A: The arrrrrrrt store.

Q: Who do Pirates call when they break their peg leg?

A: The Carrrrrrpenter.

Q: Where do pirates keep their cookies?

A: The cookie jarrrrrrr.

Q: Where do pirates put their trash?

A: The Garrrrrrrrrrrbage can.

Q: Which country do pirates like most?

A: Aaarrrgh-entina.

Q: Which famous pirate was always sad?

A: Captain Blue Beard.

Q: Which fast food restaurant do pirates like the most?

A: Arrrrrr-by's.

57

Q: Which fish do pirates love the most?

A: Swordfish.

Q: Which pirate movies can't kids go to see?

A: The ones that are rated Arrrrrrrr.

Q: Which restaurant did the buccaneer go out to for dinner?

A: Long John Silver's.

Q: Why are pirates called pirates?

A: Just 'cause they arrrrrr.

Q: Why couldn't the pirate play cards?

A: Because he was sitting on the deck.

Q: Why did the caged pirate dress up as lawyer?
A: To pass through the barrrs.

Q: Why did the pirate cross the road?
A: To get to the second hand shop.

Q: Why did the pirate go on vacation?
A: To get some ARRRR and ARRRR.

Q: Why did the pirate go to acting school?
A: He wanted a parrrrrrt in the new Pirates of the Caribbean movie.

Q: Why did the pirate move to Russia?
A: To become a Czarrrrrrr.

Q: Why do pirates always win Halloween dance contests?

A: They know how to shake their booties.

Q: Why instrument did the pirate play in his band?

A: The guitarrrrrr.

Q: Why should you never take a pea from a pirate?

A: He becomes irate.

Q: Why was it so hard to call the pirate on the phone?

A: Because he left the phone off the hook.

Q: Why was the pirate afraid of getting old?

A: He might get arrrrrrthritus.

Q: Why was the pirate ship so cheap?

A: It was on sail.

# 5

# Lunchtime Laughs

Q: Which fruit has the most whole grains?
A: The BRANana.

Q: How do apples communicate with each other?
A: With their pie-phones.

Farmer: "We're not going to grow bananas any longer."
Neighbor: "Why not?"
Farmer: "They're long enough already."

Q: Did you hear the joke about the broken egg?
A: Yes, it cracked me up.

Q: How are cereal bananas like cows?
A: They get milked every morning.

Q: How are golf balls like eggs?
A: They're white, they're sold by the dozen, and a week later you have to buy more.

Q: How are scrambled eggs like a losing figure skater?
A: They've both been beaten.

Q: How are you supposed to talk in the apple library?
A: With your incider voice.

Q: How can you tell which end of a worm is which?
A: Throw an apple and yell fetch.

Q: How did the baby banana become so spoiled?
A: Mama banana left him out in the sun for too long.

Q: How did the bread keep it's shape?
A: By spending an hour on the gym's bread machine.

Q: How did the egg get up the hill?
A: It scrambled up.

Q: How did the eggs leave the room?
A: Through the eggs-it.

Q: How did the farmer know the goat was stealing eggs?

A: The pigs squealed on him.

Q: How did the investor know Apple's stock was going to go up?

A: He had incider information.

Q: How did the unripe banana feel about the ripe banana?

A: It was green with envy.

Q: How did they describe the potato who won an olympic medal?

A: Spudtacular.

Q: How do bananas travel?

A: In a yellow submarine.

Q:  How do birds cheer for their soccer teams?
A:  They egg them on.

Q:  How do comedians like their eggs?
A:  Funny side up.

Q:  How do monkeys get down stairs?
A:  They slide down the banana-ster.

Q:  How do sweet potatoes know how many spaces to move their game pieces?
A:  They casse-role the dice.

Q:  How do you cheer up a baked potato?
A:  You butter him up.

Q: How does a penguin make pancakes?
A: With its flippers.

Q: How is a banana peel on the floor like music?
A: Because if you don't C sharp you'll B flat.

Q: How is a softball team similar to a pancake?
A: They both need a good batter.

Q: How is an ear of corn like an army?
A: Both have lots of kernels.

Q: If a crocodile makes shoes, what does a banana make?
A: Slippers.

Q: If an apple a day keeps the doctor away, what does an onion do?

A: Keeps everyone away.

Q: What can a whole apple do that half an apple can't do?

A: It can look round.

Q: What did one banana say to the other when they first met?

A: Yellow, nice to meet you.

Q: What did the annoyed apple reply when he was asked "what's eating you?" by his friend?

A: Worms—worms are eating me.

Q: What did the apple say to the almond?

A: You're nuts.

Q: What did the baby corn say to mama corn?
A: Where's pop corn?

Q: What did the bag of flour say to the loaf of bread?
A: I saw you yeasterday.

Q: What did the banana do when he saw a monkey?
A: It split.

Q: What did the butter say to the bread?
A: I'm on a roll.

Q: What did the corn say when he received a compliment?
A: Aw, shucks.

Q: What did the grandmother yam say to her grandson?

A: Orange you cute?

Q: What did the mom say to her sweet potato son when he got a good grade?

A: That's yamtastic!

Q: What did the pasta chef ride to the Hockey game?

A: A zam-roni.

Q: What did the red delicious say when it won the talent contest?

A: How about them apples?

Q: What did the sheep do after eating 20 bean burritos?

A: He went bloating.

Q: What did the slice of bread say to the other slice of bread when he saw butter on the table?

A: We're toast.

Q: What did the sport-loving sweet potato want to be when he grew up?

A: A sports commen-tater.

Q: What did the sweet potato mom like to read as a bedtime story?

A: Green Eggs and Yam.

Q: What did the sweet potato philoshopher say to the potato?

A: I think, therefore I yam.

Q: What did the worm want to do when he grew up?

A: Join the Apple Core.

Q: What did the yeast say to the bag of flour while working on their science project?

A: We Knead to be serious.

Q: What did the young loaf of bread say to the teacher?

A: Rye so serious?

Q: What did they say about the old loaf's song?

A: It's a moldy but a goodie.

Q: What did they say to the well-dressed potato?

A: You look smashing.

Q: What do bakers give people on special occasions?

A: Flours.

Q: What do bakers have to do every morning before leaving?

A: Make sure their bread is made.

Q: What do baseball players call their potato fans?

A: Speck Tators.

Q: What do corn stalk's raise?

A: Cornish Game Hens.

Q: What do corn use as money?

A: Corn bread.

Q: What do ducks like to eat with cheese?

A: Quackers.

Q: What do potatoes eat for breakfast?
A: Pota-toast with jelly.

Q: What do spiders order in Paris restaurants?
A: French flies.

Q: What do they call a bread made with gun powder instead of baking powder?
A: A POPover.

Q: What do they call stolen yukon gold?
A: Hot potatoes.

Q: What do they call the best student at Corn University?
A: The A-corn.

Q: What do they serve to drink in bakeries?
A: Baking soda.

Q: What do you call a baby sweet potato?
A: A small fry.

Q: What do you call a potato who is slow to act?
A: A hez-a-tater.

Q: What do you call a potato with right angles?
A: A square root.

Q: What do you call a spinning potato?
A: A rotate-o.

Q: What do you call a sweet potato after it's been thinly sliced?
A: Chip.

Q: What do you call an apple with gas?
A: A tooty fruity.

Q: What do you call banana motorcycle policemen?
A: Banana CHIPS.

Q: What do you get when it rains potatoes?
A: Spuddles.

Q: What do you get when you cross an apple with a shellfish?
A: A crab apple.

Q: What do you get when you divide the circumference of a yam by its diameter?

A: sweet potato pi.

Q: What kind of apple isn't an apple?

A: A pineapple.

Q: What kind of apple throws the best parties?

A: Gala apples.

Q: What kind of apples do they eat in the desert?

A: Camel apples.

Q: What kind of potato starts arguments?

A: An agi-tater.

# 6

# Silly Sports

Q: What do you get when you cross a softball pitcher with a carpet?

A: A throw rug.


Q: Why can't Cinderella play soccer?

A: Because she always runs away from the ball.

Q: At what sport do waiters do really well?

A: Tennis, because they're such great servers.

Q: Did you hear the joke about the fast pitch?

A: Oops—You just missed it.

Q: Did you hear the joke about the pop fly?

A: Nevermind. It's over your head.

Q: Did you hear the joke about the softball?

A: It will leave you in stitches!

Q: Does it take longer to run from 1st base to 2nd base, or from 2nd base to 3rd base?

A: 2nd to 3rd because there is a short stop in the middle.

Q: How can you tell if your tennis opponent doesn't like your serve?

A: They keep returning it.

Q: How do baseball players stay cool?

A: By sitting next to the fans.

Q: How do people swimming in the ocean say HI to each other?

A: They wave.

Q: How often do baseball players call each other?

A: They touch base every once in a while.

Q: What are successful forwards always trying to do?

A: Reach goals.

Q: What baseball position do spiders like most?
A: The outfield because they catch the most flies.

Q: What comes before tennis?
A: Nine-is.

Q: What detergent do swimmers use to wash their clothes?
A: Tide.

Q: What did Cinderella wear on her feet when she went for a swim?
A: Glass Flippers.

Q: What did one tennis ball say to the other tennis ball?
A: See you round.

Q: What did the baseball player do when the coach said to steal second?

A: He stole the base and went home.

Q: What did the bumble bee baseball player say after crossing home plate?

A: Hive scored.

Q: What did the maggot do at the baseball game?

A: Wormed the bench.

Q: What did the outfielder say to the baseball?

A: Catch you later.

Q: What do baseball players put their food on?

A: Home plates.

Q: What do elves play during the summer?
A: Little League baseball.

Q: What do soccer referees send during the holidays?
A: Yellow cards.

Q: What do softball players use to bake a cake?
A: Oven mitts, bunt pans and batter.

Q: What do you call a person who walks back and forth screaming one minute, then sits down weeping uncontrollably the next?
A: A football coach.

Q: What do you get when you cross a baseball player with a monster?
A: A double header.

Q: What do you get when you cross a pitcher with the Invisible Man?

A: Pitching like no one has ever seen.

Q: What do you get when you cross a tree with a softball player?

A: Babe Root.

Q: What do you serve but never eat?

A: Tennis balls.

Q: What football position do ninjas like most?

A: Kicker.

Q: What happened when the two tennis players met?

A: It was lob at first sight.

Q: What happens to football players who go blind?

A: They become referees.

Q: What has 18 legs and catches flies?

A: A softball team.

Q: What has 4 legs and grunts a lot?

A: A wdoubles" tennis team.

Q: What is a baseball player's favorite thing about going to the park?

A: The swings.

Q: What is a polar bear's favorite stroke?

A: The blubber-fly.

Q: What is harder to catch the faster you run?

A: Your breath!

Q: What is it called when a dinosaur gets a touchdown?

A: A dino-score.

Q: What is one of the rules in zebra baseball?

A: Three stripes and you're out.

Q: What kind of ants help support their football team?

A: Penants.

Q: What kind of dive are army men best at?

A: Cannon-ball.

Q:  What kind of exercise is best for a swimmer?
A:  Pool-ups.

Q:  What kind of football team cries when it loses?
A:  A bawl club.

Q:  What kind of race is never run?
A:  A swimming race.

Q:  What kind of stroke can you use on toast?
A:  Butter-fly.

Q:  What kind of tea do soccer players drink?
A:  Penal-Tea.

Q: What lights up a soccer stadium?

A: A soccer match.

Q: What runs around a baseball field but never moves?

A: A fence.

Q: What sport do tall loaves play?

A: Breadbasket ball.

Q: What swimming stroke do sheep enjoy most?

A: The baaaackstroke.

Q: What was the celebrity tennis player's favorite city?

A: Volleywood!

Q: When should baseball players wear armor?
A: When they play knight games.

Q: Where did the banana train to become a relay swimmer?
A: In an olympic-sized cereal bowl.

Q: Where did the softball player wash her socks?
A: In the bleachers.

Q: Where did the tennis players go on their date?
A: The tennis ball.

Q: Where do baseball bats wash up?
A: In the bat tub.

Q: Where do swimmers clean themselves?
A: They wash up on shore.

Q: Where shouldn't a baseball player ever wear red?
A: In the bull pen.

Q: Which animal is best at hitting a softball?
A: The bat.

Q: Which tennis tournament never closes?
A: The U.S. OPEN.

Q: Which word looks the same backwards and upside down?
A: Swims.

Q: Why are baseball games at night?
A: Because bats sleep during the day.

Q: Why are baseball players so rich?
A: Because they play on diamonds.

Q: Why are basketball players messy eaters?
A: They're always dribbling.

Q: Why did the soccer player bring string to her game?
A: So she could tie the score.

Q:  Why did the softball player go to the car dealer?
A:  She wanted a sales pitch.

Q:  Why did the teacher jump into the pool?
A:  She wanted to test the water.

# Fun Kids Jokes

## www.FunKidsJokes.com

Fun Kids Jokes is a safe resource for parents and children to find funny things to giggle at.

You'll find clean, family-friendly jokes, riddles, knock-knock jokes, videos, kids party ideas and resources to make you and the children in your life smile.

## Kid-Friendly, Parent Approved

Birthday Jokes - Unicorn Jokes - Cat Jokes - School Jokes
Sports Jokes - Holiday Jokes - Animal Jokes - Superhero Jokes
Lunchbox Jokes - Cow Jokes - Space Alien Jokes & much more.

Visit our free website at FunKidsJokes.com

Made in the USA
Middletown, DE
27 October 2018